A B C

Israel

By Rachel Raz

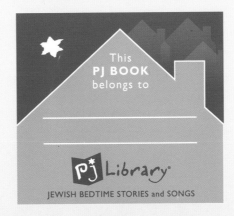

This **PJ BOOK** belongs to

_____

_____

PJ Library®

JEWISH BEDTIME STORIES and SONGS

For my parents, Sara and Nisim, who shared with me the beauty and love of Israel from a very young age.

For my husband, Gil, for his ongoing support and inspiration.

For my daughters, Daphna and Dahlia, who helped me view Israel through a children's lens.

Text and photographs copyright © 2012 by Rachel Raz

KAR-BEN PUBLISHING, INC.
241 First Avenue North
Minneapolis, MN 55401 U.S.A.
www.karben.com

Library of Congress Cataloging-in-Publication Data

Raz, Rachel.
      ABC Israel / by Rachel Raz.
         p.   cm.
      ISBN 978–1–4677–0857–9 (pbk. : alk. paper)
      1. Israel—Juvenile literature. 2. Alphabet books. 3. English language—Alphabet—Juvenile literature. I. Title.
      DS126.5.R358 2012
      956.92—dc23   2012009825

Printed in China
1 – LP – 3/20/13

A

is for almond trees

blooming in the spring.

B

is for bells

ringing in the Druze village of Dalyat El'Carmel.

C is for cats

strolling freely through the streets of Israel.

D

is for drums

nestling in a basket at the outdoor marketplace (*shuk*) in Jerusalem.

E is for egg

A girl eating an egg and *ja<u>h</u>noon* on a sunny wintery day.

F
is for figs

growing on a tree during the hot summer months.

G is for gardens

surrounding the Baha'i shrine on Mount Carmel.

H is for horses

in a riding paddock in *Moshav* Talmei-Yehiel.

I

is for Israel

as viewed from an airplane on a clear sunny day.

J

is for Jerusalem

the largest city and capital of Israel.

K is for kids

having fun in a playground in Tel-Aviv.

L is for lemons

ripening during the rainy winter months.

M

is for milk cartons

labeled with Hebrew writing.

N is for new buildings

rising in the city of Tel-Aviv.

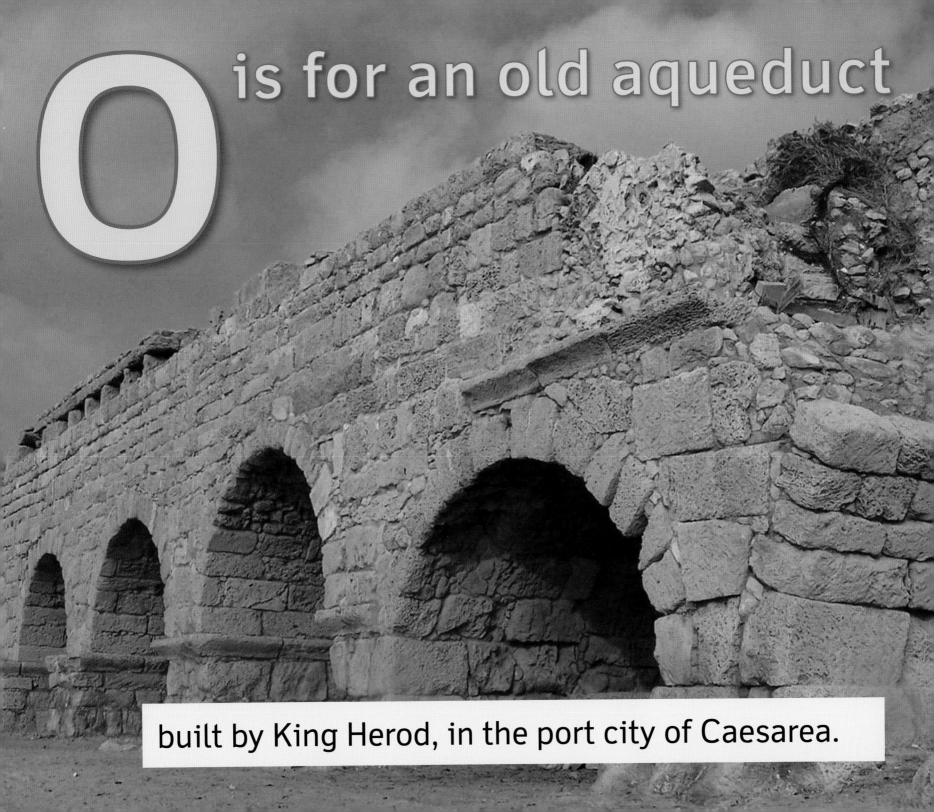

O

is for an old aqueduct

built by King Herod, in the port city of Caesarea.

P
is for pomegranates

full of red, shiny, sweet seeds.

Q is for quiet

All is quiet at the olive grove during the mid-day heat.

R

is for recycling

A plastic recycling container in the streets of Haifa.

S

is for shells

Large and small shells on the Mediterranean shore.

T

is for a taxi

driving down the streets of Ramat-Gan.

U

is for up

Solar panels up on the roofs, collecting energy from the sun.

V is for vegetables

Fresh, colorful vegetables in a supermarket in Tel-Aviv.

W is for wind

A windy-wintery day on the Mediterranean Sea shore.

X is for xylographs

Hebrew wood-carved letters spelling the word *Shalom,* which stands for peace, good bye, and hello.

Y

is for yellow wild flowers

blooming during the winter months.

Z is for zebras

eating hay at the Safari in Ramat-Gan.

Author's notes:
Like the ribbons decorating the front cover, Israel is colorful and diverse. Through the photographs, **ABC Israel** shares with the reader Israel's weather, trees, flowers, history, modern life, people, food, places, symbols, religions, languages, environmental innovations, animals, geography, modes of transportation, and much more.

Almond trees blossoming are a sign of spring. They are associated with the Jewish holiday of Tu B'shvat, celebrating the New Year for the Trees.

Bells – in Dalyat El'Carmel's marketplace. Dalyat El'Carmel is a Druze village high up the slopes of Mt. Carmel. The Druze are an ethnic group that split off from Islam in Egypt about 1,000 years ago.

Cats – in Tel-Aviv. Domestic and stray cats stroll freely all over Israel.

Drums made from clay and leather. They are also known as Darbuka.

Egg and Jahnoon. Israel's Jewish population is based on Immigrants from many diasporas, including Yemen. The immigrants bring with them their traditional food and customs. Jahnoon is a type of bread cooked for many hours.

Figs – Atzmon, communal settlement in the Galilee. The fig is one of the Seven Species Israel was blessed with according to the bible. The seven species listed in Deuteronomy 8:8 are: wheat, barley, grapes, figs, pomegranates, olives (oil), and dates (honey).

Gardens – Haifa. The Baha'i gardens, also known as the Hanging Gardens of Haifa, are garden terraces surrounding the Shrine of the Báb on Mount Carmel. The Baha'i Faith is a monotheistic religion founded by Bahá'u'lláh in 19th-century Persia.

Horses – Moshav Talmei-Yehiel. The Moshav is a type of an agricultural settlement. The first Moshav was established in 1921 . The founders dreamt of establishing a communal farming community (similar to a kibbutz) with an individual family structure. Kibbutzim had communal dining and children slept in separate housing.

Israel – Birds'-eye-view. Israel borders the Mediterranean Sea on the west. The beach is used for recreation by Israelis and tourists year round.

Jerusalem – the Western Wall (Ha' Kotel, the Wailing Wall) is located in the Old City of Jerusalem at the foot of the western side of the Temple Mount. It is a remnant of the ancient wall that surrounded the Jewish Temple's courtyard, and is one of the most sacred sites in Judaism.

Kids – Tel-Aviv. Playgrounds can be found in every neighborhood.
Although Israel suffers from a shortage of water, thanks to several innovations, well developed irrigation systems keep the country and its playgrounds blooming and green, without waste.

Lemon tree – Ramat Ha'Sharon. Israel is known for its citrus fruits and in particular the Jaffa oranges. For many years oranges were the number one export product from Israel. Israel has since come a long way and in the 21st century Israel demonstrates its ability to compete on the global stage in a broad range of industries .

Milk cartons labeled in Hebrew. Hebrew and Arabic are the two official languages in Israel. English has a semi-official status and is used extensively at all levels of society.

New – Tel-Aviv is a modern and vibrant city. Known in Israel as The City that Never Stops. It attracts many tourists as well as many Israelis, especially young people.

Old – The old aqueduct system in Caesarea is one of many archeological sites in Israel. The systematic archeological investigation of the country's past has uncovered sites ranging from prehistoric times through the end of the Ottoman rule.

Pomegranates – Atzmon. The Pomegranate is one of the symbols traditionally used on Rosh Hashanah, the Jewish New Year. Eating pomegranates on Rosh HaShanah is a symbol of hope that the coming year will be full of good deeds as many as the seeds of the fruit.

Quite in the olive grove – a view from the Muchraka, south-eastern peak of Mount Carmel.
A great location for a panoramic view of Jezre'el Valley and the southern Galilee.

Recycling – Haifa. Since the mid 2000s, Israel's Ministry of Environmental Protection has focused its efforts in promoting recycling.

Shells – Caesarea beach.

Taxi – Ramat-Gan. Public transportation is highly developed in Israel. It is easy to get from one place to another using buses or trains. In cities taxi rides are common as well.

Up – Haifa, a view from the Baha'i Gardens.
Israel is a pioneer in the use of solar energy. Almost every residential building in Israel uses solar panels to provide hot water. Many street lights are powered by solar energy and solar panel farms are being constructed all over the country.

Vegetables – Vegetables grow year round in Israel and take an important place in the Mediterranean diet. In restaurants vegetable are included in every meal including breakfast.

Wind – Winter winds attract para-surfers to the shore.

Xylographs – Tel Aviv, an arts and crafts stores. Xylographs are wood carvings. Unique art supplies related to the Jewish holidays and symbols can be found in crafts store all over Israel.

Yellow – Wild flower carpets grow during the winter months even in the arid desert. Israel's plant life is rich and diverse, in part due to the country's geographical location at the junction of three continents. Some 2,600 types of plants have been identified.

Zebras – Ramat-Gan. The "Safari" in Ramat-Gan is a home to many animals foreign to the Middle-East. Thanks to the comfortable conditions it is common to see new born babies strolling around.

Rachel Raz in an educator, a photographer, and a traveler who frequently visits Israel, where she took all of the photographs featured in this book.